WIN! WIN! WIN!

Keys to Relentless Resilience

-What I Have Learned from My Patients-

Stella Lin

In remembrance of

My grandmother

Ah-Sha Chen

To my children

Andy, Rosie, and Joyce

"I can do all things through Christ

Who strengthens me."

Philippians 4:13

CONTENTS

INTRODUCTION

I am a psychologist. In the past 22 years I have been providing services mainly in health care facilities. Most people are aware of the fact that people of faith are in a win-win situation when they are critically ill. If they live, they win. If they die, they have eternal peace, and that is a win too. But the truth is, if you have unshakable faith, you are not only in a win-win situation; you are in a win-win-win-win-win……. situation. You simply cannot be defeated.

This principle is not only true for people who are dealing with health issues; it is true in every challenge in our lives. To have unshakable faith is to be PERMANENTLY POSITIVE. With this attitude, we are shaped to be winners regardless of our circumstances. We are relentlessly resilient. We are destined to have victory.

As a psychologist I have the privilege to cheer my patients on when they make their journeys and fight their battles. I have the opportunities to access the inner parts of their hearts and their minds. I have learned so many valuable lessons. I am indebted to all of them as my precious teachers. That is why I feel compelled to share what I have learned with other people, people that I cannot reach in my psychology practice, people who are in great distress but do not know how simple it is to turn their lives around.

I have had the desire to write this book for a long time. In recent years the sense of urgency has been intensified. It appears that so many people are unhappy in this world. Some people seem to have accepted life as a journey of a series of sufferings, and death as the final relief. They are barely surviving, not truly living.

If you are not shooting for the best, you will not get the best. No matter what kind of situation, there is a best life possible for you to obtain. You have what it takes to be a winner.

In this book I am going to explain to you why I say so.

It is my intention to combine the simple but powerful principles of spirituality and psychology to empower the readers. I am a Christian; therefore, I am writing as a Christian. However, I do hope that people who are not Christian would also be willing to read this book and benefit from it. It is also my hope that this book may be helpful to mental health professionals, medical professionals, and health care workers of all kinds as I share my experiences of working with my patients. I know we all work together as a team.

1

GET STARTED BY COUNTING YOUR BLESSINGS

The first thing I want to say is that it is easy to get started. Right now in your life you may have many concerns and worries. You may be in real trouble. Some problems may be external, coming from the outside to attack you. Some problems may be internal, coming from inside of you. You may feel overwhelmed and powerless. If you try to tackle one problem, the possible solutions may be tangled up with other issues. You also notice that things seem to be all connected. One bad thing leads to another. There is a never ending vicious cycle. You just feel you cannot win.

The good news is: there is also a positive cycle. If you choose one positive thing to do, you will also find that one good thing leads to another. You will discover a positive cycle in motion. Over time you will be amazed by what unfolds in front of you. If you can think of one good thing to do, go ahead and do it. In addition to that, I would recommend that you get started by counting your blessings. You may think this is not very exciting or creative. Let me give you some examples to show you how this simple action can be life changing.

Twenty four years ago, I worked in a state psychiatric hospital as a psychology intern, an ABD (all but dissertation), a student in training, a novice. At the time I was also a baby

Christian. I started working there only a few

months after I was baptized. I am telling you

these stories to show you that it does not take

rocket science or complicated theology to

overcome difficulties in your life.

At that hospital I was assigned to treat a

woman who repeatedly tried to commit suicide.

They told me she had been admitted to the

hospital every month or two, sometimes only a

couple of weeks apart, for many years. She just

would not stop trying to end her life. One of my

supervisors told me to take this patient for a

walk on the campus ground every day and talk

with her. She told me about her loneliness

since her parents passed away and she had no siblings or children. She told me about the past traumas she endured in her childhood and her youth. Regardless of difficulties she experienced in the past, she was able to acknowledge that there had been many positive things she also enjoyed over the years. Our conversations always ended with a natural sense of gratitude. Nobody really wants to die. Paralleled with every suicidal thought there is a yearning for life. When the time came for her discharge, I had her write down things she was thankful for on index cards to take home. It was a simple project of counting her blessings. She recalled some of our conversations. She added some more. To make them more interesting, she also decorated them, using color pencils. I remember there were statements such as, "I am grateful I live in the United States of America." I guess talking with a graduate student from a foreign country gave her a new perspective. There were simple things like, "I am thankful for the sunset. I enjoy it every day." According to another supervisor whom I kept in contact with over the years, this woman never returned to the hospital again. We are made to live. We are created to enjoy our lives.

I remember there was another patient at that hospital, who was admitted also due to a suicide attempt. When we had a counseling session in the glass booth on the admission floor, I helped her acknowledge that there was an encouraging voice in her mind. I asked her to let that positive voice encourage this down-hearted woman in her. Once she started, words just flowed out of her mouth. She said things like, "You are a good person. You really have a lot to live for. You are still young. You have a good future. It would be a shame if you give up......." As her own words moved herself to tears, I saw healing taking place.

Just like my patients, you have what it takes. It is an innate ability that God gave us to count our blessings and encourage ourselves. This simple mechanism has great power.

"Count your blessings, not your woes." "A joyful heart is a grateful heart." We all know these old sayings of common wisdom. But we do not actually take action to do it. There is a difference between a vague sense of thankfulness and a solid, deliberate, intentional attitude of gratitude.

You may be thinking, "How am I going to count my blessings when everything goes wrong in my life?" Just do it. And God will help you continue.

I remember the first day when I started working in the nursing homes as a psychologist. I was almost in a shock to be face-to-face with people who were suffering from severe illnesses and disabilities. Suddenly I felt short of means to help them. I knew my encouraging words were not sufficient to comfort and empower my patients. I immediately decided to pray with them. And I immediately witnessed the power of God through our prayers together. I regained my confidence until I went to a room to visit a woman who was a stroke survivor. She was completely debilitated. She was unable to talk but her comprehension was intact. They referred her to me because she was suffering from severe anxiety. When I saw her, she was literally trembling and shaking. After talking with her by talking for her and obtaining confirmation through her nodding and shaking of her head, I felt she was ready to tackle her problem. To coach her how to remit her anxiety, I held her hands and prayed with her. I counted her blessings with her, big and small. To be honest, I felt sorry for her and I did not even know what to say. But once I started it came out on and on like a chant. "Thank you, Lord for saving my life." "Thank you, Lord for this day." "Thank you, Lord for the beautiful sunshine." "Thank you, Lord for my family and the love we share." "Thank you, Lord for my doctors." "Thank you, Lord for the nurses and everyone who is helping me." "Thank you, Lord for healing me. I am a little stronger and better every day." I was surprised that I did not run out of things to say for her at all. After a few minutes of chanting and praying, she completely stopped trembling. When I wrapped up our prayer and opened my eyes, I saw her face in front me, smiling with calm delight.

When you actually search your heart, soul, and mind to identify what you are thankful for, not only that you will not run out of things to say, you may be surprised by what you come up with. Before I did my internship, there was one year I worked in a federal prison for my practicum as a graduate student. I had an inmate on my caseload who was attending meetings of Alcoholic Anonymous. He was very motivated and was making good progress. He confessed to me that he stumbled on the issue of spirituality. As a nonbeliever at the time I used the common sense and suggested for him to start by counting his blessings. A week later he brought a long list to our counseling session. On top of his list of blessings was the prison. Yes, indeed, the prison was his number one blessing. He told me how the prison gave him the opportunity to change and grow. It was an inspiring experience for me to see how God opened his eyes. I knew it was not me. I was amazed, especially when I thought about how more than 50% of the new inmates told me during the admission intake interview that they were wrongly convicted and should not be incarcerated.

Are there things that are blessings to you and you just have not seen? Every one of us has many, many blessings. Too often, we are just blind. Are you in a place that you do not want to be and yet it is actually a blessing for you to be there for the time being? Are you blind to see the divine purpose in a challenging situation? The action of counting your blessings may give you new awareness and insight.

So, put the book down for a few minutes. Close your eyes and think about what you have just read. Think about for what you are thankful. If you need to do some chore, this is a good time to go do it. While you are doing the dishes or laundry, walking the dog, working out, or taking a walk, count your blessings one

by one. Experience the peace and joy the

attitude of gratitude produces for you.

2.

DISCOVER THE POWER OF PRAISE

I believe it was not hard for you to count your blessings. Don't you feel better already? The attitude of gratitude is highly valued in every culture; therefore, most people are familiar with it. As I grew up in Taiwan I learned and tried to practice this attitude of gratitude. I remember there were at least two articles about attitude of gratitude in our elementary school textbooks. But my patients have taught me a whole new level of such attitude and the power it brings.

I would never forget this lady who was on dialysis due to end-stage renal disease. When we prayed together I always let her go first. Every time she started her prayer with this statement, "Dear Lord, everything about you is good and perfect." At first it almost puzzled me. How could she say that? She was on dialysis! We did not know how long she would live! And coming to live in the nursing home was heart wrenching for her! This lady showed me what it meant to praise and worship in all circumstances. And I witnessed the power of such sincere praise. I learned why she was able to enjoy the recreational activities and make new friends even when she was dealing with severe medical issues. When it was her time to leave this world, she went into deep and peaceful sleep for many days. I saw her face in her sleep and I was sure she was not in any pain or distress. It was apparently a peaceful transition from this life to eternal life.

There have been many other patients who showed me how to praise God in the midst of sufferings. One lady always started her prayers by saying, "Dear Lord, thank you for this day and the goodness in it." A gentleman said this all the time, "Thank you Jesus! Praise your name!" A lady who had 26 surgeries in her life time said, "Lord, you are so good to me!" One lady with terminal illness sat in her death bed and told the nurse's aides every day, "Isn't God so good?!" I am telling you about them, but to be honest, there is no way I can really convey the profound impact of inspiration they gave me.

Let me make an attempt to share with you what I have learned. Ironically, like a miner who found precious gemstones deep in the dark underground cave, I found the secret to obtaining a fulfilling and enjoyable life in the face of pains and sufferings, death and dying. I still cannot fully express what I mean. Here is another try. In other words, my patients while in their pains and sufferings taught me how to be winners simply by praising God.

There were times in my life I found myself in the situations like the sky was crushing down on me. One example was when my ex-husband told me that he wanted a divorce. Have you ever had so much pain that you did not know what to do? I did not even know how to pray. Then I thought of these patients. I did exactly what they did all day that day. I had to go to work and I had to encourage my patients although my heart was bleeding. I thanked God for being with me. I praised God throughout the day whenever I had a moment. I sang songs of praise on the way home. The next day I started singing a new song I made, "Everything about you is good and perfect......" Yes, those were my patient's words. Since then

I have made many songs of praise. It amazes me because I have no musical background. I don't know if I would ever have the opportunities to share those songs with other people, but one thing I know for sure is that over time God turned my moaning into dancing; He turned my sorrow into joy. (Psalm 30:11) I am sharing this very personal experience with you because I know many readers may be going through a divorce, separation, or breakup.

A painful breakup is not the only situation that may make a person feel like the sky is crushing down. A diagnosis of terminal disease, a sudden disaster or injury, a sudden loss of employment, sudden death of a loved one may all make people feel that way. Are you in one of those situations? Some people say they just feel numb. It may be difficult for you to do anything. But you have just counted your blessings. You have done a great job.

Once you have calibrated an attitude of gratitude you are ready to take the next step. It is indeed true that you will feel better right away if you tell yourself for what you are thankful. Now bring your blessings to God and thank Him and praise Him for what He has done. You don't need to say long prayers. Do what my patients did, expressing gratitude with a line of sincere acknowledgement. You will discover an explosion of power in your spirit and a shield

of protection in your soul.

Starting in the next chapter I am going

to teach you some psychology principles that

will really help you. But there are good reasons

that I show you these basic spiritual principles

in the first two chapters. Because they are not

just life changing; they are indeed life saving.

Nothing is more effective to stop the bleeding

of the heart and start the healing of mind, body,

spirit, and soul than praise and worship.

Remember that praise is a lifestyle, not

just an occasional incidental action to please

God and get what we want. Be grateful not

only toward God, but also toward people. Do not be reluctant to show appreciation to others. How easy it is to take God for granted! How easy it is to take people for granted also! When we have a lifestyle of praise, we are setting an atmosphere of peace, joy, and love around us. Don't you agree that is a win already?

3.

MAKING THE DECISION AND TAKING A STAND

By this time I believe you have already experienced something good happening inside of you. Before moving forward, I would like to invite you to make a decision and take a stand to be a winner. It is important to position yourself in your mind before you tackle your problems. I did not learn this in graduate school. I learned it from my patients in various settings. After visiting with me for a period of time, they would tell me that they had decided to be happy. It amazed me that they literally told me that they had "decided" to be happy.

Indeed, even if you have a wonderful counselor giving you compassion and support, you still need to decide to be happy. Even if you are on antidepressant medication, you still need to decide to be happy. Even if you go to church every Sunday, you still need to decide to be happy. Otherwise, you will not be happy. It is easy to forget that no matter what contributed to our conditions and situations, we are still holding a big switch in our own minds. We are still in charge.

It may be necessary for you to go over what you have been through. You may need a good cry. You may need to dump out some junk and clean out the closet of your emotions.

But at the end of the process do not just sit in a

puddle of tears and indulge in self-pity. Never

review your past sufferings without seriously

acknowledging your resilience. After playing a

video clip in your mind, be sure to resave the

memory with a side note that says, "But I

survived it." Furthermore, take a moment to

thank God and praise Him for making you

stronger. By doing so, you are claiming the

strength that you gained which you might not

recognize before. I am telling you my trade

secret here. I do this all the time. I do not need

to give my patients strength. I just help them

acknowledge what they have already had.

Once they owned what God had already given

them, they would rise up to apply the gifts in every aspect of their lives.

The real problem with human minds is that we tend to save our memories of traumatic events as traumatic events, not as records of survival and victory. One time I was sent to visit a patient in a nursing home who was extremely nervous about a scheduled surgery. She told me that she had cancer and also severe heart problems. Three years earlier she was diagnosed with cancer. Her doctor said that if they operated on it she might die on the operating table because of her heart problems. So the doctor recommended to just monitor her cancer. But during her recent checkup her doctor informed her that the cancer had

progressed to the point a surgery was required

in order to save her life. She was terrified by

the thought that she might die on the operating

table due to her heart problems. It was such a

dilemma. I asked her what surgeries she had in

the past. She named four, some were major

surgeries. She talked about them in details and

how she recovered from each and moved on to

her life. We praised and thanked God together

for what He had done for her. I did not have to

tell her. She concluded at the end of the

session that this surgery was no different from

other surgeries she had before. She

acknowledged that there was a risk but she was

ready to take the risk. I reminded her there was

always a risk for any surgery for anyone, and that was why the hospitals always asked us to sign a bunch of papers. What happened a week after was amazing. As soon as I walked in the facility, I saw her sitting behind a table as one of the volunteers doing fund raising bake sale for the activity department. That was truly a rapid recovery.

I believe everyone can relate to the story that I have just told. Can you see now? You have what it takes. I have said it before and I will say it again. You just need to claim it, own it, and use it. Let me tell you another story of how someone made a decision and took a stand to win.

At the federal prison where I did my practicum as a graduate student I was treating a Vietnam War veteran who suffered from post-traumatic stress disorder. He told me about his horrible experiences during the war and how he won many Medals of Honor without feeling honorable. He had a recurrent dream. In the dream an army recruiter would tell him he was going to Vietnam to fight again. After having counseling with me for a few months he became more lively and positive. One day he told me he had decided to be happy. I asked him if he would like to get rid of that dream. He agreed to tackle it. So he practiced what to say to the army recruiter when he had the dream next time. At first, I pretended to be the army recruiter. Then I let him play the role of the recruiter and I pretended to be him. Eventually he was able to talk to an empty chair, switching freely between the roles of the recruiter and himself. That was a fun session. I reassured him that he would be able to refuse to go back to the war when he had the dream again. Guess what, after a week, he came in and told me he had the dream, and he simply told the recruiter, "I'm not going. I've already served the country." I worked there for one full year. This veteran did not have that dream again during the time I worked there.

You may be thinking, "I am in a worse situation than that man." Let me tell you about this lady who was sent to the nursing home to die. She was fully aware of her terminal status and she was on Hospice. I was sent to help her go through the dying process. She was the one who revolutionized my idea about life and death. She was a devout Christian. I helped her review her life and thank God and praise Him for her blessings, hoping the sense of fulfillment and thankfulness would help her die in peace. She laid in bed for a couple of weeks. Then she got bored waiting to die. So she asked for physical therapy. She was told that if she wanted to do physical therapy, she could not be on Hospice. She had to choose between the two. She chose physical therapy. She chose life instead of death. And she got better and better.

All her medical issues were either resolved or stabilized. After a few months she was well enough to participate in recreational activities. She went on many field trips and went out to eat in restaurants with the group. She was well enough for me to discontinue my service. She lived for more than 10 years until it was truly her time to leave this world. Because of her example, I learned not to make any assumption about a patient's future. And sure enough, I have had the privilege to witness many miracles. I will share some of them with you in later chapters.

So make a decision and take a stand now. Tell yourself that you are not going to give up. No matter what it takes, you are going to

do your very best with a cheerful spirit. I would

like to redefine the old saying, "Hope for the

best; be prepared for the worst." Imagine the

best, and work toward your vision. Also

imagine the worst, and tell yourself that even in

the worst scenario you are fully equipped to

fight and win victory. You may need to get your

loved ones on board also, so that you can all be

on the same team.

A very common mistake is to imagine

the worst scenario, thinking that way in case if

you do not get what you really want, you will

not be disappointed. Some people even believe

that if you think you are going to get the very

best, you will jinx it. Be careful about what you say. Here is another example which revolutionized my idea about life and death.

This lady was getting old and it was no longer safe for her to live alone. She was never married and had no children. After a fall her niece sent her to live in the nursing home with the doctor's recommendation. She was not happy about it. So every day she said, "I'm gonna die." She walked with the walker. She did not have major medical issues, only some age-related functional decline. But she would spit every fifteen minutes throughout the day and say intermittently, "I'm gonna die." She was sent for a thorough examination of her throat and her lung. No problem was found.

She continued to spit and say, "I'm gonna die."

They sent her to have a complete whole body

examination and did the whole nine yards, e.g.

blood tests, MRI, you name it. No problem was

found. So they sent me to visit with her. I tried

to help her acknowledge that she was in a fairly

good health. I found that she was a Christian.

So I also prayed with her at the end of each

session. After our prayer, she would

immediately say, "I'm gonna die." I told her not

to say so. But she would not stop. Guess what

happened, after less than two months, she

suddenly died without any sign in advance.

Note that she did not say, "I want to die." or "I wish I would die." It did not seem like she desired to die. That is the scary part. Don't say negative things you don't want. Also remember, faith without a good attitude is not sufficient to help you, especially if you are prophesying a bad future. Because by doing so you are making a negative decision and taking the wrong stand.

I believe you get it now. Put the book down and say a simple prayer. I am confident that this suggestion would not offend most readers. Almost every one of my patients told me that they prayed whether or not they had a religious affiliation. Isn't that something?

Almost everyone is connected with God. Even if you have never done it, you can start now. You can say it out loud or say it silently. No one else has to know about it. Tell God you know that He will guide you and empower you along the way. Tell Him you have made a decision to be a winner. Tell Him you have no fear because you know you are in this together.

4.

SETTING THE RIGHT MINDSET

I want to remind you that you have done a good job to get the basics. Before you read this chapter, take a moment to tell yourself, "Good job! Keep up the good work!" Be prepared to see the level of your confidence come up higher and higher. In this chapter I want to tell you another simple but powerful tool that can change your life. Let me start with a story of one of my patients.

This middle-aged woman came to the nursing home to do rehabilitation after her discharge from the hospital. She had a rare disease with a very long medical name of which I had never heard. She was paralyzed from her waist down. She told me that it was genetic and her mother had it. For several weeks she made no progress and she was very depressed. It appeared that she might eventually need long-term care placement. I got on the internet, trying to get more information to understand this rare disease. The information confirmed what the patient told me that her white blood cells were attacking her neurological system. As I ran through various sources, I came across two research articles in which both indicated that the condition was reversible, even in the titles. Suddenly the word "reversible" was flashing in front of my eyes. I printed them out and showed them to the patient when I visited her. I sang the Christmas tune, "Do you see what I see?" She said softly in amazement, "It's reversible!" I gave her the papers and said, "Yes, it's reversible! Hang on to it! Look at it! Think about it! Get it down to your system! It's reversible!" We prayed together and thanked God for putting this information in our hands. We received God's healing with gratitude and joy. I also made sure that the primary care physician got a set of the articles and the information that this patient's condition was reversible. I requested extended physical and occupational therapies on her behalf. Since then the patient made tremendous improvements. She was discharged to home after a couple of months.

Can you see that the key to successful recovery is in your mind? This patient had the same body, the same doctors, and the same therapists before and after that crucial moment when she changed her mindset from hopeless to hopeful. The optimistic anticipation propelled her to make genuine efforts for her therapies, resulting in a positive outcome.

Let us review this case for a few more moments. As a psychologist, when I got online to look for information concerning that rare disease I was not only looking for general information, I set out to look for something I could use to encourage the patient. Again, I am telling you my trade secret here. Before I see each patient, I always review the medical records and talk with the staff. I am not only trying to get information about the patient, his/her medical issues, history and background, patient's personality and attitude, family and support system, etc., I am actively and intentionally searching for things I can use to encourage/empower the patient. This habit is so built-in within me that I am almost like a rescue dog searching for the scent of disaster survivors who are buried under the rubble. What is my point in telling you this? If I were not looking for positive information, the word "reversible" would not have flashed in front of my eyes. It would not have rung a bell. You too have to cultivate a habit of looking for positive things to encourage yourself. Otherwise, even if God presents signs and wonders in front of you, you would still be blind to them.

I would like to insert a side note here. If you had a major sickness, injury, or surgery, chances are that in addition to healing from the damage of your body, you are also fighting for recovery from disuse atrophy. The common saying is true that if you don't use it you'll lose it. The good news is if you use it again you will gain it back. That is why the loss of functioning can seem so scary at first, but people can recover beautifully. I have a very good friend who has a son that had severe pneumonia one winter. His breathing difficulty was so severe that the doctors put him in an induced coma in order to get rid of his pneumonia. After a month his pneumonia was completely cleared. When he was revived from the coma, he could not do anything at all. He had to learn everything all over again by doing physical, occupational, and speech therapy. And he completely recovered after a few months. I am telling you this not to scare you, but to encourage you that many of your body's functions will return.

Another thing I want to highlight here is: the importance of team work. Notice that I did not keep the positive information to myself. I shared it with the primary care physician and requested extended physical and occupational therapies for the patient. Keep in mind that you do have a team behind you and you have a strong influence on people on your team. Your team may include medical professionals, family, and friends. I often tell my patients to share their progress with their loved ones, because they need encouragement too. When your team members are positive and optimistic they feed this positive energy back to you. Then you get a positive cycle going here for your own benefits. Too often, the person who is sick or going through a difficult life situation makes everyone feel sad and depressed like he/she is, and they just help one another be more and more down-hearted. Remember you can change it by starting to be optimistic yourself and rub it on them.

The same principle applies if your challenge is that someone you love is seriously ill. Getting down and depressed is not the best way to show your compassion and concerns. Point out to the person whenever you notice improvement, even if it is very small. The more you love the person, the more you need to stay strong and not to get burned out. Bringing hope and optimism to the person is what is truly helpful. It will also energize you.

Very few people are optimistic by nature. For most people it requires intentional efforts. And it is true that it is easier said than done. That is probably what you want to say to me now. And I agree. Let me tell you my own experience of struggling to be a winner.

I started writing this book near the end of 2016. Soon after I finished the first three chapters, out of the blue I fell and fractured my right wrist. My bones broke into several pieces. The doctor looked at the X-ray picture for 5 seconds and immediately recommended surgery without examining my wrist. He declared to me that I would never get well without a surgery. So, it was that bad. I am right handed. Having a surgery would make me completely disabled with my right hand for quite a while. I asked the doctor, "If I have a surgery, will I be perfect?" He said, "No." So, I asked the doctor, "If I don't have a surgery, will I be able to drive again?" He said, "Yes." One month later I saw another doctor for second opinion and still got the same recommendation. Basically, without surgery my wrist's range of motion might compromise after the bones healed. Surgery might bring a better result but still not a perfect recovery. Surgery also had many risks and would definitely cause multiple problems for me in terms of activities of daily living. I almost wished I could live in the nursing home for a while after the surgery. But I was not allowed to do so. Therefore, after weighing the pro's and con's I decided not to have a surgery. All I got was a soft cast. I told my patients about my injury. One patient and her roommate said to me, "You are one of us now." They were exactly right. I realized it was hard to live what I preached. It was very hard to maintain an optimistic mindset, especially when the doctor told me that I would never get well without a surgery.

Today my wrist is completely functional and its range of motion is still improving. How did I pull it through? I knew from the beginning that complete healing for orthopedic injuries generally would take about a year. So, I was prepared for a long haul. When people saw me wearing the cast, many of them came out and told me about their own experiences of injuries and recovery. I realized that orthopedic injuries were much more common than I thought. Their stories greatly encouraged me. With or without surgeries, they all got well. I selected two examples of recovery without surgery to constantly use as my reminders. One example was a lady who worked as a housekeeper in one nursing home. She had a wrist fracture a year earlier. She had no trouble doing all the physical works required by her job and she had no pain. The other example was a 92-year-old patient. She fell and fractured her wrist many years earlier and had a complete recovery. Not only that, she did not have arthritis of any kind. Those two examples were deeply wired in my brain.   They were my weapons to destroy negative thoughts. And of course, I did all the things I have told you in the first three chapters, thanking God and praising Him, celebrating every small victory along the way.

The truth is, for most people the road to recovery is not a smooth highway. Most likely, it is like an up-and-down zig-zag journey. Therefore, if you know somebody who has overcome what you want to overcome, do what

I did. Use the successful example as your vision to cheer yourself on.

If you cannot think of anyone as your role model, get on Youtube and search for testimonies of recovery from your issues. You will find many examples. Remember you want to get well and be an inspiring example for others. Frequently after being asked doctors would tell the patients the chance of their recovery based on statistics. Statistics is meant to give professionals understanding of the risks of the condition. It can be very misleading for people who are seeking recovery. It is based on what happened in the past. It does not necessarily predict the future. And it has nothing to do with you as an individual. If the doctor tells you that 75% of the people with your condition got well, tell yourself that you are going to be one of the majorities. If the doctor says that 75% of the people did not get well, tell yourself that you will be one of the minorities. You can be one of the people who change the future statistics. If you really think about it, there is no single disease or medical condition that completely defeats every person who has it. There are winners in every situation. And you can be one of them if you set your mind to be one.

In every disease there is a condition called "in remission." It means that the disease becomes inactive and not affecting the person's health. I have witnessed it over and over throughout the years. Our health care system typically is quiet about it. Medical professionals are trained to focus on problems, resolving them, and moving on to the next patient. They are busy all the time. Nobody would jump up and down to celebrate when someone's condition goes into remission. That is why you don't hear about it very much. And most of the times doctors do not discuss the chance for remission with the patients. That is why it is very important for me to bring it to your attention. Indeed, there is always hope.

Sometimes healing comes when the person changes his/her mindset not about the disease or condition only, but about the whole picture. Imagine that you are in a concert or are watching a stage play. It is kind of like the difference between before and after the stage lights are turned on. Or have you seen how the moment the color of the lights changed, the whole stage was transformed?

I used to do independent medical examination for workers' compensation cases. One woman suffered from post-traumatic stress disorder after an elevator accident. She worked as a security guard in one of the skyscrapers. She was in the elevator alone late at night when the elevator suddenly went out of order, rushing from the 50th floor down toward the ground in a very fast speed. Suddenly the elevator stopped between the 10th and 11th floors. In her panic she soiled herself with urine and feces. She had to wait for hours until she was rescued. Since then she had nightmares every night. She was a Christian believer. She admitted she was thankful that she was alive. But she also wondered why God allowed all these horrible things happen to her. I told her that I thought she took God all wrong. I pointed out to her that if an elevator was out of order, wasn't it supposed to fall all the way down to the ground? Why did it suddenly stop after falling down so many floors? Wasn't that amazing?   She whispered, "Um, I've never thought about it that way.   That's right.   It's amazing."   What was really amazing was that after a year when I did the annual re-evaluation with her she completely recovered from PTSD, anxiety, and depression.   She was also enrolled in college, trying to advance her career.   I did not do extensive counseling during our evaluation time.   All I did was spending one minute to help her change her mindset from being upset with God for His abandonment to being grateful for His rescue.

This reminds me of a young man I met at the airport one time.   I was there to pick up my younger daughter.   He was waiting to pick up a friend and he sat right beside me, doing his phone. I could smell alcohol even though I was not facing him. I chatted with him to kill time. He told me he was 28 years old and he owned a computer consulting company. He had twenty some people working for him. After accepting my sincere compliments for his great accomplishments at such a young age, he asked what I did. I told him I was a psychologist. He said that he envied me. He believed with my line of work I must have a better sense of meaning and purpose for my life. I told him that I did love my job, but certain things about my job he probably would not like. I then pointed out to him that his business was contributing to the country's economy. He was creating jobs, supporting not only his employees but also their families. How wonder that was! And it was still growing. How exciting that was! Suddenly he jumped up and said, "I've got to go. My friend has arrived." After a few minutes he returned with his friend. He looked like a different person with a cheerful spirit. He said that he just wanted to come back to thank me. I encouraged him to keep seeking God, for he told me earlier that although he did not have a faith background, he would read the Bible when he felt down-hearted.

I have never seen that young man again; therefore, I cannot tell you exactly how he was later on. I am using him as an example just to illustrate the technique of changing a mindset from negative to positive in the way that may be easy for you to understand and master. I believe that was a life changing moment for him to discover that he did not have to change his life or to search every corner of the world in order to find meaning and purpose for himself. By the way, the subject of meaning and purpose is very important and I will discuss it further in later chapters.

After reading about the examples I have told you, can you identify the areas you need to work on in changing your mindset? If you turn on the right switch, it may take only a moment. Try the techniques you have learned so far. Do not worry if you cannot fully execute the transformation. We are going to talk about this some more in the next few chapters.

5.

ZOOM-IN AND ZOOM-OUT

It may be quite easy for you to see how to set the right mindset when I was telling you the stories of others in the last chapter. But when you try to apply it in your own life, it may be still hard for you to get a handle on it. That is because we function much better in our thinking and problem-solving when we are objective. A big obstacle for us when we are in trouble of any kind is that we become extremely problem-focused and self-focused. This obsession may distort our perception and also interfere with our thinking process. There are several ways to overcome this natural

human tendency.

Let us talk about problem-focused

obsession and how to restore the right

perspective first. To help you understand what

I am showing you, I would like you to do a

simple exercise. Pick up your cell phone to

represent the problem you have in your life.

Hold it in your hand and look at it. What

happens is that as you get more and more

concerned and worried you pull your problem

closer and closer to your attention. So, slowly

bring your phone closer and closer to your face.

Notice how your phone looks bigger and bigger,

although in actuality it remains the same size.

Continue to do so until it covers your eyes.

Now, all you can see is the dark screen of your

phone. You cannot even tell it is a phone. And

you cannot see anything else in the room. Do

you see what I am getting at? Isn't that exactly

what you have been doing to yourself? You get

overwhelmed by a distorted perception about

yourself, your life, and your problem. The

picture you see right now is totally not the true

reality.

For most people, after the initial stage

of astonishment they will naturally restore their

perception in order to function properly. What

you have just done was like a zoom-in. This

mechanism is destructive when it blocks your view. Many of my patients were able to break away from doing that when they became aware of what they were doing. But there is another kind of zoom-in which is actually beneficial. If you turn on your phone and go to Google Maps, you can zoom-in to locate the specific address you are looking for. You can see the location of the place in relation to the surrounding neighborhood in details. That is the kind of zoom-in you may need to do.

After I finished my internship I got a job at a crisis center in a nearby city as the program manager of a women's program while I was working on my dissertation. The program provided individual and group counseling for victims of domestic violence. I often had to help the women examine themselves, their childhood and youth, their past traumas of sexual and physical abuse, their dysfunctional family of origin, etc. Throughout the process we did not just zoom-in to examine, we acknowledged their resilience as well. I helped them change their identity from victims to survivors, to victors. I would ask them, "What have you learned from your experiences?" An experience is only an experience if you do not process it. That is why people often repeat the same mistakes over and over. Every experience, good or bad, can be a learning experience if we are willing to learn. It enriches your life and makes you stronger and better. When we get to the roots of the problems, there is a long-lasting result of healing and transformation. I worked there for two years until I graduated, completed one-year post-doctoral supervised experience, and then passed my licensing examination. After I left that job, on several occasions I ran into my previous clients. They told me how well they had been since they finished the program.

The benefits of zoom-in are the most significant for survivors of childhood sexual abuse. I have worked with them in all various settings, outpatient clinics, my private practice offices, psychiatric hospital, prison, skilled nursing facilities, and assisted living places. Many people had never told anyone about it. I would tell them, "You have just given yourself justice by telling me about it. It takes tremendous courage and strength to do so. You should be very proud of yourself." By bringing the secret out from darkness, they disabled the power the traumatic experience had over them.

What is really problematic is when someone gets stuck in a zoom-in mode without productively processing current and/or past experiences. Like the way you were holding your phone to block your view without turning the phone on, you may dwell on your problems without examining or understanding them. To unstuck yourself you need to take intentional action to zoom out. Let us go back to where we left off of that exercise. Pick up your phone and cover your eyes with it. Then, slowly pull it away from your face. Your world is no longer all dark. The phone looks smaller and smaller. You can see all other things in the room. You can see the sunshine coming from the outside through the window. You can see your cat or dog or your family members. Remember we were talking about counting your blessings, thanking God, and praising God? That is an action of zooming-out as you become fully aware of positive things in your life. Instead of telling me about their problems, my patients would tell me about their families, friends, and things they enjoy in life. I would affirm their notion that they are truly blessed and I would reinforce their sense of thankfulness. Your problem is not the only thing you have in life. It is important not to ignore it. It is also important not to magnify it.

I have to tell you about a dream one of my friends had during a difficult time in her life. She was going through a divorce and seeking employment after staying home with her kids for years. In her dream she saw three gigantic boulders standing on the ground. She tried to push one then another, running among the three rocks without any success of moving them.

Suddenly she saw a huge hand coming down from the sky, moving from the horizon toward her. All three boulders were taken by that hand. In that huge palm of the mighty hand, the three gigantic boulders looked like the size of three little peas. This dream enlightened her greatly. You can see the spiritual and psychological implication/interpretation of this dream. That was a wonderful example of zoom-out which occurred while my friend was asleep. We might not have this dream. But we all need to be reminded how small our problems are in God's hand.

To zoom-out is to look at the whole picture. So far we have discussed how to do it

83

in the context of space. To break the problem-focused obsession, we also need to look at the whole picture in the context of time. For example, after processing their pains and heart-aches with the domestic violence survivors, I would ask them to imagine how big of a deal these traumatic experiences would be to them when they were 80 years old. They would pause and think for a moment and reply, "It is not going to be a big deal anymore." This common saying is very true, "Time will heal." It was so wonderful to see the courage, hope, and confidence my clients displayed regardless of the inerasable memories of traumas.

Talking about time, there is one thing I want to alert you. Life is a series of events and time flows like a river. For most people the journey of life down the river is a combination of joy and sorrow, exciting surprises and horrible disasters, and everything in between. But when I asked my patients to review their lives, most people agreed that usually things turned out fine even after a period of suffering and struggle. Believers would declare that God never failed them. And certainly, I reinforced that perception. If you section the time line in a positive way, you will find that all things work together for good. But if you section the time line in a negative way, you may easily conclude that your life is nothing but a series of trouble;

when one trouble subsides, another is rising on the horizon. Therefore, calibrate in your mind and section the time line of your life with a positive attitude, and you will find that just about every story has a good ending, although sometimes it happens sooner, sometimes it takes a very long time.

A positive attitude not only helps us to section the time line of our lives positively, it also helps us connect various events in a meaningful manner. For example, many tragic events gave birth to well-known charitable organizations. Note that connections of events may not be linear. Quite often, if you connect all the dots, a complicated net would be revealed. When you see the amazing

connections, you may be moved to tears.

Indeed, we know that all things work together

for good to those who love God, to those who

are the called according to His purpose.

(Romans 8:28) I have experienced that many

times myself, often many years after the events.

When we see that, we are zooming out and

seeing a greater picture. Such revelation also

tells us that the picture may continue to expand.

This is not the end of your story.

I bet some of your experiences are

coming to your mind and your heart now.

Don't you feel so blessed and grateful? Don't

you feel some of the things are so incredible

that they must be God's works? He has done it many times before and He will do it again and again. No one can take this confidence and such deeply rooted peace and joy away from you.

6.

SHIFTING ANGLES AND CHANGING POSITIONS

We have discussed how to break the
problem-focused obsession. Now let us talk
about ways to break the self-focused obsession
which also interferes with effective thinking and
problem-solving abilities. To illustrate this I
would like you to do another simple exercise.
Select an object to represent your problem. For
safety's sake I would not recommend using your
phone. Grab a water bottle instead. Examine
the object from all angles. You will find how
different an object looks from different angles.
The most extreme is that if you look from the
top or bottom of a bottle, it does not look like a

bottle at all. If you look from the very top, you can only see a small circle (the cap) sitting inside a bigger circle. What happens when we are in a crisis is that we are more likely to get stuck in one position in our perception. We abandon our ability to shift from different angles by freely changing our positions to observe.

I always enjoy chatting with my coworkers in the break room. People would talk about their problems. I am often amazed by the wise advices given by others. It is so much easier to come up with ideas when you are in the position of a bystander. This is why I sometimes ask my patients, "What would you say to someone who is in your situation? What would you say to encourage him/her?" This is especially effective if they used to be in a profession of guidance, such as teachers, pastors, nurses, nurses' aides, social workers, etc. I am always amazed by how easy it is for my patients to come up with something to encourage themselves just by a simple shift of angle and gentle change of position in their minds. You may try this too. Ask yourself what you would say to encourage someone in the same situation.

In the outpatient setting, sifting of angles can be easily done by using an empty chair. One time I had a client who had issues with his mother and he had not seen her for several years. What brought him to my office was his difficult relationship with his wife. At first, he told me about both relationships in a fragmented manner. I told him we were going to try something that might help him. I asked him to pretend to be me and imagine he was sitting in an empty chair. I asked him, "As a psychologist, what would you say to this man who is asking for your help?" Within a couple of seconds, he said to the empty chair, "The problems you have with your Mom are affecting your relationship with your wife. Don't be stubborn. Go visit your Mom." This man never studied psychology. In fact, he never went to college. Isn't that amazing? I took away the empty chair and asked him, "So, what do you think about this advice?" He said, "I'm going to visit my Mom this weekend." So, I said, "Sounds like a good idea. You've got nothing to lose anyway, do you?" After he restored his relationship with his mother, his marital relationship greatly improved. Totally he only needed a few counseling sessions.

Another interesting phenomenon is that most of the time I do not even have to question them about what they would say to encourage someone in the same situation. All I need to do is to provide them a safe and comfortable atmosphere. They would just pour out their hearts and tell me everything that comes through their minds. When people receive empathy and compassion they need, they immediately feel better. Then they would say things to encourage themselves. All I need to do is to affirm what they say and reinforce their positive thoughts. I am not a researcher. My guess is that when people are talking to me they are listening to what they are saying also. In a sense, while they are listening to their own speech, they are changing their position from themselves to somewhat like a third-party position. This gentle and natural shift of position helps them break the self-focused obsession and gives them new insights. They are no longer stuck. Their minds are lubricated and they are free again to examine their situations from all angles. Like what I have told you, you've got what it takes. I do not need to give you anything new.

Here you can see the benefits of having professional counseling. If you need it, do not be afraid to get it. In the last chapter of this book I will give you some tips about receiving professional counseling. Talking with a trusted friend or family member is also very helpful. Another thing you can try is journaling. In the process of writing, you are thinking and exploring from various angles of perception. One thing that is very important about journaling is not to make it a rampage of complaints and indulgence of self-pity. It is ok and healthy to vent, but be sure you write

something to encourage yourself and always

wrap up with positive thoughts. Remember to

thank God and give Him praise. Over time your

journal will become a documentation of the

fingerprints of God and your personal testimony

of His power and His love.

When it comes to shifting angles and

changing positions, there is no better position

than seeing things in God's eyes. When we

follow God, He helps us see things differently. I

saw two new patients right before Christmas

last year. Both of them told me they went to

church in their childhood. They both accepted

my prayers at the end of our sessions. I did not

have any theological discussion with them. After that I took time off for the holidays. Subsequently we had unusually cold weather with sleet and bad road conditions. Finally, I went to work, but they had quarantined that section of the facility due to the flu virus. So, I did not see those two new patients again until over a month later. When I asked for updates of the patient who was reportedly negative and critical, they told me he had been "like an angel." When I talked with him he told me how God had been helping him. I went to see the other new patient. Amazingly she told me how she appreciated support and love her family had shown her all her life. I clearly remembered how she complained about her family during our first session, accusing them for doing things for her only out of obligations. What a big change of perception! Not only that, she had changed from a taker to a giver. She told me that her family took her out to eat in a restaurant and she insisted on paying for the meal to thank them for being so good to her all those years. Because of my extended absence, I can confidently tell you that their mind change, attitude change, and behavioral change, all have nothing to do with me. The only variable was that they both reconnected themselves with God. That is what I am going to talk about in the next chapter.

7.

PLUG IT IN

Just the thought of writing this chapter is making me feel excited. The biggest thing I have learned from my patients in the past 22 years is the power of faith, exactly what I did not learn in graduate school. I am still learning more about it today and I know God will continue to teach me and amaze me. What happens to a lot of people is that when they are scrambling to deal with crises they forget to plug in with God. Even believers can be so overwhelmed and do not notice that their faith is not plugged in. No wonder they feel totally powerless. But once they plug it in, they can freely receive God's power.

Last year I saw a patient who came to one facility for short-term rehab after having a heart attack. On top of the recent heart attack he had end-stage COPD (chronic obstructive pulmonary disease) and was on oxygen 24/7. He also had contracted a severe infection and was on IV antibiotics. He had severe anxiety and depression, so severe that he did not want to be around other people. Therefore, instead of going to the therapy room, he received physical and occupational therapies in his room. Considering his age and his multiple medical issues, many workers suspected that he might need long-term care. When I went to see him

for the first time he was restless and anxious. I

encouraged him just as I had encouraged other

patients. At the end of the session I asked him

about his faith background. He stated that he

went to church when he was a child. I asked

him if he believed in God. He shrugged his

shoulders without saying yes or no. I asked him

if he would mind that I prayed for him. He said,

"Not at all." So, I held his hands and prayed for

him just as I prayed for other patients. One

week later, he was a totally different person

when I went to see him. He was no longer on

oxygen. His infection was cleared. Instead of

trembling in bed, he was sitting peacefully in

the armchair, watching TV. I asked him how he

made such tremendous progress within a week.

He replied, "You just have to trust God." Wow!

He then told me that they were talking about

discharging him. A week later, he was no longer

there. It was an eye-opening experience for me.

I am so glad I offered prayer even though he did

not say that he believed in God.

You just need to plug it in. You don't

need to have great faith. Once you are plugged

in, the Divine power will flow through. I had a

patient who was dying from HIV. That was

what the staff told me when they made the

referral. They sent me to see him because he

was angry at his situation and had some

behavioral issues, being verbally abusive toward

the staff. He told me he grew up in a bad

neighborhood. There was a church that sent a

bus to pick up the kids around his neighborhood

every Sunday and took them to church. He said,

"I never missed a Sunday." It was one of the

very few positive memories he had. When he

became a teenager, he stopped going to church

and started doing drugs. He got HIV from

shared needles. After telling me all the trouble

he had as an adult, he went back to talk about

his childhood experience of going to church.

His face was beaming with joy. He said that he

still believed in God. I asked him if he was ever

baptized. He said that his parents were never

involved, so he was never baptized. He got

excited when I told him he could be baptized by

the Chaplain. The Chaplain at that facility was also the Activity Director. He told me that since the patient had no family support, he would perform the baptism in the dining room and make it a special event. That way the patient would have support from other residents. I thought it was a great idea. But the Chaplain was so busy every day and the baptism was delayed continuously. In the mean time, this patient just got better and better. Anyone could see he was no longer dying. And he no longer had behavioral issues. One day while he was resting in his geri-chair in the hallway, the Chaplain walked right by him. He reached out his hand, grabbed the Chaplain, and asked, "When are you going to baptize me?" The

Chaplain said, "I can baptize you right now if you want." So, he was baptized there right on the spot. After the baptism the patient continued to recover. After about a year, he was walking with restorative therapy aids, using a walker. That was his condition before he was transferred to another facility. I am laughing with joy as I am typing to share this story with you.

Here is another example. This lady had cancer which metastasized to her spine. The first time I saw her she told me she was a Christian believer but she had not been in church for many years. She cried when I held her hands and prayed with her. I could feel she was not crying out of sadness. She was

somehow deeply touched by God. After a week,

she told me she felt better. She said, "Look."

Then she got out of her wheelchair. Very

quickly she held on to the furniture and walked

wobbly for three feet. I did not even have time

to push the call button for help. I told her to sit

back down and be careful. She then told me

that at the hospital three doctors told her she

would never be able to walk again. She said,

"But look, I can walk now!" I encouraged her to

keep working hard with the physical and

occupational therapists. We praised God and

rejoiced together. This time when we prayed

together, I was the one who cried. Three

months later she was discharged. As she

described it, "Not only can I walk; I can dance!"
With my encouragement, she came back to
work as a volunteer for the Activity Department
until she moved out-of-state. She not only
recovered physically, she also recovered
mentally. When I initially got the referral, I was
told that the patient was "a little off," as she
verbalized delusional thoughts. I recommended
not to jump the gun. Since her so-called
delusional thoughts did not appear to be
harmful to herself or others and she had no
past history of psychosis, I suspected that the
symptoms might diminish as she progressed in
her recovery and antipsychotic medication was
probably not necessary. Sure enough, she
became as normal and cheerful as could be.

Isn't that amazing? Want to hear another story? This lady actually had a long history of mental illness. As she became older she had multiple medical issues. With the doctor's recommendation she was placed for long-term care. Her family urged her to accept it. The staff told me that she had been crying and demanding to go home every day since her admission. They also told me about her "goofy and crazy thoughts." When I went to see her, she was shaking and trembling. She said in tears, "They told me this is it." In addition to her long history of mental illness and her current multiple medical issues I found that she also had a long history of being a devout Christian growing up in the South and living there most of her life. I told her that the facility

was not a prison and she was not sentenced for

life. But pounding on going home would not

work. Judging from her current condition, her

behavior would convince people even more

that she had no common sense and could not

make decisions for herself and she definitely

needed to be here. I helped her see why she

indeed needed to be at the facility for the time

being to get well. I suggested for her to go to

God instead of going to people to put in her

petition. But once she put in the request to

God, she really did not have to nag God

anymore. I encouraged her to cooperate with

physical and occupational therapists and get

better and stronger each day. I reminded her to

thank God for His help and praise Him for her

progress along the way. She did that faithfully.

Not only did she get better and better physically,

but her anxiety, depression, and goofy thoughts

all went away. She did not need any assistance

anymore. She could walk, take a shower, dress

herself, and she even made her own bed. After

a few months, she beat all the odds and went

home with confirmations from all medical

professionals. A year later she came back to the

facility. This time she was not referred to me

for psychological services. Apparently she did

not need my help. I happened to see her when

I passed by her room. She told me she fell and

injured her leg. I told her she must be doing

very well because no one asked me to talk with

her. I said, "God has healed you before; He will do it again. You have done this before; you can do it again, right?" She smiled and said a loud "yes." A few weeks later she went home again.

How are you feeling now? Are you pumped up? Are you plugged in? Sing a joyful song!

8.

PRINCIPLE OF ACCUMULATION

I hope you enjoyed the testimonies I gave you. The great majorities of people do get better and are stabilized in health care facilities. It is very rare for people to just get worse and pass away after their admission. In a sense, just about everyone is receiving God's healing and miracles. Certainly, it is even more so outside of the nursing homes, but in most cases the process may not be so dramatic. Therefore, I think it is important that I cool you down a little here.

Even among the examples I gave you in the last chapter, did you notice that although it only took me one paragraph to describe each story, in most cases it actually took place over a much longer period of time? What I notice is that it is a lot easier for me to see my patients' progress than themselves, the staff, and their families. The reason is that I see them only once a week. The rest of the people see them more often. The worst observers are usually the patients themselves, because they are with themselves all the time. It is kind of like when I was raising my kids. When we got to see our relatives, they would point out that the kids grew so much taller. But I did not see the dramatic difference, because I was with them every day. I used to measure my kids' height and make a mark on the wall each time. They loved seeing the visible records of their growth. Since my patients do not keep visible records of their own progress, I have to help them review their growth marks.

If you do not feel that you have made much improvement, think hard. Do not compare your current condition and situation with the way you were before the crisis occurred. Compare your current condition and situation with the way you were when the crisis just occurred. You will see that you have come a long way. You may still have a long way to go. But if you keep going to the right direction, you will get there.

Things add up. Think about it this way.

You don't even have to suddenly get a lot better.

If you just get a little better each day, you will

get 7 a-little-betters in a week. That will add up

to 30 or more a-little-betters each month. In 3

months you will accumulate more than 90 a-

little-betters. -- And that is a lot better! This is a

funny way to put it. But don't you think it is

very true?

In addition to the principle of

accumulation, I also notice the phenomenon of

acceleration. The journey of recovery is usually

difficult and slow at the beginning. I often feel

that it reminds me of an airplane, slowly moving

on the runway at first, then it runs faster and

faster. Suddenly it takes off in the air. After a

while it climbs up higher and higher until it

reaches the targeted altitude. Then it flies

stably. I have observed this kind of pattern over

and over again.

So, do not be discouraged if you are at

the beginning stage and things are going slow.

Know that it is normal. Keep doing what you

are supposed to do. Keep celebrating your

little-betters. Keep counting your blessings.

Keep thanking God and praising Him. Take one

day at a time. Live one moment at a time.

Keep plugging it in. No matter how long it takes,

you will reach your goal.

This gentleman did exactly that. He came to one facility to die. He had untreatable cancer in the spine. If they operated on it, they could have killed him. So, he was on Palliative Care, a program for people who were dying slowly from terminal conditions. His wife was already living there, because she had Alzheimer's disease. He was suffering from severe pain and side effects of his medications. There were times he saw things that were not there, although he knew they were not real. He lived in the same room with his wife, but she was unable to be his emotional support at all. He had very strong faith and a positive attitude. He just kept going. One winter his wife had a cold which turned into pneumonia. They rushed her to the hospital. Within a week she passed away. On top of his sufferings he had to grieve for her sudden death. But he just kept going. We prayed together. He praised God for what He had done for him throughout his life. Slowly, he got better and better. One of his legs had been amputated several years earlier when he was initially diagnosed for cancer. He had a nice prosthesis. When he was so sick he just let it stand in the corner in his room. But when he felt better, he started to put it on, trying to walk again. When the staff noticed his motivation, the team decided to give him physical and occupational therapies. They strengthened his body first. Then he was able to stand, wearing his prosthesis. He started to walk with a walker, then with a cane. Little by little, he got better

and stronger. He participated in recreational

activities. He went out to eat in the restaurants

and went on field trips with the group. He went

target shooting with his long-time friend.

Eventually he was able to walk simply wearing

his prosthesis. He was able to go back to his

church and attend the service every Sunday. A

lady who worked at the kitchen volunteered to

accompany him. By this time, he was totally

symptom free from terminal cancer.

In the health care facilities there is a

system to monitor each patient's condition,

progress, needs, and treatment goals. Staff

members from all departments work together

as a team. They attend the morning meeting every morning. They have care plan meetings scheduled for each patient weekly, biweekly, monthly, or quarterly, depending on the patient's condition. The patient and his/her family are invited to the meetings. There is a registered nurse (RN) who is responsible for compiling MDS (Minimal Data Set), recording measurable information concerning each patient's functional level, improvements, or decline in every aspect of the patient's health.

I am not done with the story yet. As this gentleman got so well, there were no longer discussions about his pain and suffering. Nobody was talking about his cancer anymore.

Instead they came to him and told him that if he would like to get an apartment and live in the community, he could do that. What a nice surprise for an 82-year-old man! He got his cats back from his daughter and moved to an apartment. Two weeks later I ran into him at the facility. He told me that he kept falling at his apartment. Although he did not have any injury, he was thinking it was not a good idea for him to live alone. So, he picked up the phone and asked if he could come back. He was glad he could. He continued to enjoy his life as much as possible. He resumed his hobby of collecting airplane models.

Do you agree that this man got a miracle from death to life? But guess how long it took for this miracle to be fully revealed? Three and a half long years! Not all miracles are instantaneous. Don't be blind to the miracles God is unfolding to you by getting a little better each day.

This patient was truly my hero and my teacher. I no longer work at that facility, but he is still living there, alive and well. I remember one time I told him how inspiring he was to me and how I used him as an example to encourage hundreds of my patients. Suddenly, he burst into tears. He said, "Don't praise me. Praise God. He's the one who did it all." He asked me, "Have you seen a movie called 'God Is Our

Copilot'?" I said, "I've heard about it. But I've never seen it." He said, "That's wrong. God is our pilot. We are His copilots." I said, "You are right. I've never thought about it that way." Don't you think he was the one who should get paid for that session, not me?

He was basically telling me his secret. It is hard to persevere when it takes a very long time and your improvements are not leaps and bounds. A lot of people get out of shape. I have seen patients who wanted to get well so badly they gave themselves anxiety and depression. I have seen patients who gave themselves more anxiety because they were afraid they could not get rid of their anxiety. I have seen patients who gave themselves more depression because they worried about their depression. Do you know how easy it is to give yourself this kind of bonus? If you don't do anything about it, it can go on and on. This wise man points to us a great solution. Let God guide us and just cooperate with Him. He is the pilot of our lives. We are to be good copilots. As you are making progress, you are also dealing with the unknown future. You may not even know what to ask from God. God's way is higher than our ways; His thoughts are higher than our thoughts. (Isaiah 55:8-9) He blesses us above what we may ask or think. (Ephesians' 3:20) What a precious gift to have peace along the way as you get better and better.

9.

FLIPPING AND RESETTING

Now we know it is so important to keep
calm and carry on. Does it mean you will always
do that? What can you do if you suddenly get a
setback? How do you fight back if you get
discouraged? It is more likely to happen here
and there when the healing process takes a long
time. Sometimes, people may do very well for
months and suddenly get depressed. It is
almost like combat fatigue that some soldiers
have. Keep in mind that a battleground is also a
holy ground. The difficulties you go through do
not foreshadow defeat; it will only add intensity

of joy to your final victory, and consequently, glory to God.

In the real estate business there is a special kind of investment. The investor would purchase a rundown foreclosure property at a very low price, fix it all up, and sell it for a great price. It is called "flipping." That is exactly what you need to do. But don't get overwhelmed. You do not have to remodel your brain or squeeze it. Isn't that good news? To do flipping in your mind is as simple as flipping a piece of paper. Or think about it like a computer. All you need to do is to click or touch on that little arrow, and it will take you back to the last page. If you have worked on making a positive decision and setting up the right mindset I have told you in previous chapters, you have already built a structural foundation in your mind. Your efforts were not in vain. It should be easy for you to reset the right mindset without rebuilding it. The main thing is that you need to catch yourself when you are getting negative. Sometimes negative thinking can be subtle. We may gradually stray away from the right path without knowing it.

I want to remind you how powerful your mind is. You may have heard a lot of talking about the power of the mind from scientists, researchers, doctors, and preachers. I have too. But to see some extreme examples among my patients was eye-opening. I had a

patient whose brain was damaged by a stroke.

She had the stroke when she was only 43. So,

she thought she was 43 all the time. She was

66 years old when I met her. And she looked

like 43. Regardless of her disabilities caused by

the stroke, she had no grey hair, no wrinkles at

all. The same thing happened to a male patient

who had a stroke when he was 57. He thought

he was 57 all the time. He looked like 57. He

acted like 57 when he was 75.

That was shocking, wasn't it? We are

what we think we are. Be careful about what

you think. Don't tell yourself you are not

getting any better. Especially watch out for

what you say to yourself and others. I have found it to be very true that words have even greater power than thoughts. To think is one thing; to speak it out is another level higher. Every time you say something, you are calibrating your brain and you are shaping your reality. That is why I would say to my patients, "Tell me all the good things that happened in the past week." As they talk, they are listening to their own speech, reviewing their progress, and foreseeing further improvements. They are encouraged by their own words. They are resetting the positive mindset. Have you noticed that it is hard to say one thing and think the opposite at the same time? Try it, and you will know what I mean. It will make you feel like your brain is about to pop. By saying positive things, you are gently forcing your mind to line up with your words. If you do that, you can catch your fear right on the spot and change it into faith, turning defeat into victory.

You may want to say that you are capable of having positive thoughts but negative emotions at the same time. I know what you mean. It is true that it often takes longer for our feelings to catch up with our minds. I have seen many patients who made rational decisions to stay in the long-term care facilities. They knew it was the right decision, but they still had to go through the process of grieving for losses and making adjustments. I have also seen many patients who hold up a

positive attitude concerning their disabilities

but still had to grieve for their losses of

functioning, independence, their possessions,

and body image, etc. It takes time for my

patients to accept their new normal and take

actions to make the best of it. The biggest

problem for human beings is that we are not

robots. It is not like things can be set and done

once and for all.

Let me encourage you with a story. A

couple of years ago I had a coworker whose

daughter was pregnant with a set of twins. It

was a joy at first, but soon a horrible situation

occurred. The doctor found that one of the

twins died. If they removed the dead fetus, they might hurt the living baby. So, her daughter was instructed to carry the baby full-term together with the dead fetus. Can you imagine that? Grandma (my coworker) was devastated. I prayed with her and encouraged her to bring the positive attitude to her family. Another coworker cautioned her that everyone in her family should welcome the baby with joy when she arrived and truly enjoy her as she grew up without allowing her to live in the shadow of her dead twin sister. Truly words of wisdom! The daughter went through such a difficult pregnancy and gave birth to a healthy baby. This wonderful family made it through together. They buried the dead baby and

moved on to raise the precious surviving one.

This is a very rare situation. But if you

take it as an analogy, everyone can relate to it.

We all have some broken dreams, like the baby

that died. Have you ever met anyone who has

never had any disappointment or loss in his/her

life? I have not. On the other hand, we have all

experienced that when one dream died,

another dream was emerging, although we

might have to carry both for quite a while until

the new dream was born. And how wonderful

it is when the new dream is fulfilled. We

become more thankful and we cherish what we

eventually have. Remember, do not let your

new dream live in the shadow of the broken

dream.

We just have to be like those inflated

punching toys. When we are punched and fall

down, we will come right back up. I will never

forget this lady who had 26 surgeries in her life.

She was a double amputee. Both her legs were

removed way above her knees. She also had a

colostomy bag, because her colon was removed.

With physical and occupational therapies she

learned to hop on a board to transfer herself

from her bed to her wheelchair. She did that

every day and emptied her colostomy bag

herself. It was just unbelievable for me to see

her motivation to maintain maximum

autonomy. But one particular day she had such

severe pain she was crying throughout our visit.

She was not due for her Morphine until a

couple of hours later. She told me that her

surgeon was suggesting to trim her stumps one

inch further to possibly remove the pain. As we

were wrapping up our visit, it was time to go

down to the dining room for lunch. After our

prayer, I pushed her wheelchair. Together we

sang, "Onward Christian soldiers, marching as

to war. With the cross of Jesus, going on

before......" I still feel that heart-wrenching

feeling as I am typing right now and I am trying

very hard not to cry, exactly what I did that day.

But you know what, when I saw her a week

later, she greeted me with a smile again like she

always did. This lady is one of my greatest

teachers. After working with me for a few

months she was transferred to another facility

to be closer to her family. But over the years,

every time when she came to my mind I felt a

powerful combination of emotions; the heart-

wrenching pain and great joy of gratitude would

overwhelm me again. I did not know where she

went, but I knew she was somewhere, inspiring

people around her like how she did to me.

A real winner is not someone who

never cries in pain. When you cry in pain, don't

think that you have lost the game. A real

winner is someone who never gives up. A real

winner is someone who keeps going and keeps

singing along the way even with tears in your eyes and pains in your heart and your body. It is in darkness where the light shines brighter. Let your light shine. Let the light of God shine through you. You are serving God in your sufferings. Nothing is more powerful than that for others to see.

So, how do you do the flipping and resetting of your mind? At the very beginning of this book I gave you my favorite verse from the Bible, "I can do all things through Christ who strengthens me." (Philippians 4:13) There were times in my life I had to say this to myself repeatedly to pull myself back on the right track. I would also say, "In Christ I am more than a conqueror." (Romans 8:37) Try it yourself. And

don't forget this one, "This is the day the Lord

has made, we will rejoice and be glad in it."

(Psalm 118:24) Hey, now you can keep going

and keep smiling again.

10

DON'T ASK WHY

Another thing that can lead you off track is the question "why." Why did this happen to me? Why am I the only one in my family who has this disease? Why did this accident happen? Why did this disaster happen? Why, oh, why? Do you know why I title this chapter "Don't Ask Why?" Have you seen this poster I like? On the top of the poster it says, "Anti-stress Kit." There is a big circle at the center which says, "BANG HEAD HERE." Below the circle there are detailed instructions. I love this poster but I have never given it to my patients. I gave it to some coworkers and we

laughed about it together. This is why I tell you
not to ask why, because you will be banging
your head against the wall. You are not going
to get anywhere.

One time I had a contractor who came
to my house to fix something. When the work
was done we sat at the kitchen table so that I
could write him a check. He told me that a year
ago during a family cookout one of their
grandchildren, a toddler, tripped and fell and
died. No, he did not know that I was a
psychologist. People would tell me about their
problems for no reasons. He said that his whole
family had been depressed over this terrible
accident. He wondered how long it would take

for them to get over this, or perhaps they would

never get over this. A year had gone by, but

they did not feel any better. I told him that

happened to one of my friends. Her mother

tripped and fell and died. It also happened to a

lady who lived in a nursing home, simply

because a man in the wheelchair jokingly

pretended to run her over. The family actually

sued the facility. But this man and his family

could not sue themselves. Sensing how he

desired to get out of this painful grief but did

not know how, I then told him what I called

"the Parable of the Bird Poop." I parked my car

outside of the garage and some bird pooped on

the windshield. It was a big splash of poop. I

regretted parking outside, but the bird poop

was already there. It would not go away by itself. Even if I prayed to God, it would not go away by itself. The only way for me to get rid of the bird poop from my windshield was to pick up the hose and wash it off. That was what I did. Somehow this weird parable I made up resonated with him. He brightened up and thanked me. He said that he would go home and tell his wife about it.

As you can see, people have the question of "why" not only about themselves but also about their loved ones. That is just as hard if not harder. Years ago I had a patient whose daughter committed suicide. Her family attempted to protect the patient by not letting her know. She finally found out several months later. But she did not attend the calling hour, funeral, or burial. Her grief and distress were so great that she not only became deeply depressed but also seriously ill. She passed away within a couple of months.

On the contrary, I had a patient who also had a daughter that committed suicide. It hit her hard at first, causing her depression and physical decline which brought her to be placed for long-term care. She was a woman of strong faith. She never asked why God did not stop her daughter from killing herself. She just kept doing her best. When she felt better she tried to encourage other residents. She participated in recreational activities. She tried to enjoy the birds that came around the feeder outside her window. On her good days she went out to eat in the restaurants with the group. She volunteered to deliver mail to the residents and give them greetings. She made friends and she prayed for people who were sick. She told me that she realized that God put her there at that facility for a purpose. I do not work at that place anymore. But she is still living there, alive and well.

Can you see how this lady picked up the hose and washed off the bird poop from her windshield, so to speak? And it was good that she faced her disaster head on. The other lady's family meant well, but shielding the

person from distress probably made it worse.

Yes, you need to face your problem head on.

When you do that, you are not banging your

head against the wall; you are breaking the

obstacles like a bulldozer and heading toward a

better future. Yes, I am saying a better future.

Here is a good one to share with you. I

had a patient who told me that she was mad at

God that she had cancer. She knew that God

did not give her cancer. But the thought that

God allowed it to happen to her just made her

very upset. Why didn't God protect her? As

she reviewed her life during our visits, she

admitted that God had been very good to her.

She did not find the answer to her question, but she was at peace with not having an answer. The simple action of counting her blessings worked like living water washing off anger and resentment in her heart. I am glad you notice that we are going back to chapter one, Count Your Blessings. That is indeed the basic. An amazing thing happened as she resolved her bitterness. She told me she had less physical pain and the doctor reduced dosage of her Morphine. A month later, she told me she was completely free of pain and no longer taking Morphine. She was then discharged to home. I did not know if she became cancer free later or not. But the fact that she became free of pain was a big lesson for me. I believe it is a big lesson for you too.

Don't ask why. Just count your blessings, thank God, and praise God. Let God heal you and empower you. If you keep doing these, you may find the answer to your question one day. I have told you about my wrist fracture. As I recovered, along the way I discovered how beneficial the experience was to me. I have found myself cherishing everything more than before. I was so happy and thankful when I pushed the trashcan down the driveway for the first time after many months. It made me cry when I drove again, just around the neighborhood. It was like going to paradise when I drove to Walmart for the first time, freely shopping without considering the limited time my driver could spare for me. What a blessing to be able to wash my back! What a blessing to be able to wash my hair with both hands! So many times I seemed to be making progress, then my wrist, hand, and arm swelled up and hurt after I challenged myself to do more difficult tasks. I had to tell myself that it was a setback, but I did not go all the way back. After doing flipping and resetting of my mindset, I waited for the swelling to subside, then I started therapeutic exercise again. I declared victory in Jesus when I no longer needed to grab a stranger in the grocery store and asked, "Would you be so kind to break up my bananas for me?" Just a month ago, I finally opened a bottle of water by myself without wearing rubber gloves. I wanted to dance and celebrate all day. For more than a year I had to ask someone, "Would you be so kind to open this bottle for me? I had a wrist fracture." Now I understand better when my patients say how much they hate to ask for assistance. Now I realize how shallow my empathy for them was. And I know I still don't really know how they feel and probably never will. I wrote the first three chapters of this book before I had the wrist fracture in December of 2016. I resumed this project in early 2018. When I finished my first draft and went back to review the first three chapters, guess what, I didn't like my writing! Certain parts were almost irritating to me. I had to rewrite and change a lot. I realized the experience of a wrist fracture had changed me profoundly.

The experience of suffering and struggling has many benefits. It increases faith in God, humility, gratitude, compassion, wisdom, coping skills, sense of humor, to name just a few. After being broken and made whole again, we become less defensive and more real. We also become less offensive and more considerate. If you hold up a positive attitude, I can guarantee that you will reap the harvest. And perhaps the harvest will be the answer to your question.

There are certain situations that you do need to ask why, not to God, your family, or your friends, but to your doctors and yourself. No, I am not going to confuse you at all. I have seen many patients who ruined their health by alcohol and/or drug abuse. It is interesting that most of them did know their medical issues were caused by their addiction. I knew that chronic exposure to those harmful chemicals could damage liver and kidney. I did not know they could also cause strokes and heart attacks until several patients told me so. I got online and checked on NIH's website (National Institute of Health.) Sure enough, it was confirmed, even marijuana could cause strokes and heart attacks. If you keep fixing your medical issues without getting rid of the

addictions, your health will continue to

deteriorate. Obesity is similar to that. A lot of

people have a host of medical issues caused by

their obesity, but they have never connected

the dots. In these situations, not going to the

root of the problems will actually keep you

banging your head against the wall. You not

only need to ask why, you may also need

professional help. I will give you some tips in

the last chapter of this book.

11.

ALTRUISM

This is a very important chapter. That is why I use this fancy word as the title to catch your attention. In my opinion, altruism is the most essential ingredient for victorious living. Altruism means the philosophy of benefiting others. It is the total opposite of being selfish and self-centered. Common sense tells us a person cannot be happy without the desire and action to benefit others. This concept is honored and promoted in the traditional values of every culture. It is the core of Christian faith also.   Altruism is shown in love, friendship, hospitality, consideration, kindness, compassion, sacrifice, charity, empathy, heroic deeds, advocacy of justice, etc. It is what makes life worth living. It is what brings the kingdom of God to the Earth. It is what gives us sense of meaning and purpose. Yes, meaning and purpose, I did not forget I promised you to talk about that. It is what is called love in the Bible. But this love is not quite the same as what people call love. It is love without selfish motives.

Without it, you can have the power to hold the whole world in your hand and still feel the void inside. Human beings are social animals. We not only need to be connected with others, we also need to feel that we are benefiting others in order to have a sense of fulfillment. Why am I having a philosophical discussion now when we are getting close to the end of this book? I have learned from my patients that such love is what makes us real winners. Therefore, I would like to remind you not to abandon it while you are struggling to overcome difficulties in your life. Without such love, even if you become healthy, strong, and problem free, you will have no joy.

To make it simpler, let us just call it love. When we love, we are serving God by serving others. Life is ultimately very short. When it is boiled down, at the end of the day, what really matters is love. Love is the only legacy that we can leave behind when we are gone.

Love in action does not have to be big projects. I had a patient who lived in a nursing home and had multiple medical issues herself. But she always stayed on top of what was going on with her family and friends. Indeed, moral support is more powerful than physical presence. She was always there with them through good times and bad times. When someone lost his job, someone had an injury, someone lost a loved one, and she consoled them and encouraged them. When someone got a job, someone got married, someone had a baby, she shared their joy with them. She lived for many years regardless of her imperfect health. Her love for others kept her going. And she was surely missed when she passed on.

Love can be carried out by small actions. The smallest one I remember was one of my patients who faithfully changed the date display on the wall every day for years until his last day. He did it because he knew it was important for the residents to keep track of dates. It became his mission. Some patients served in the Welcome Committee. They went to visit new comers, bringing gift baskets, friendship, and encouragements. One lady crocheted lap blankets as gifts for new residents. I have a patient now she crochets little crosses to give away. She also crocheted Easter baskets and dressed them up to give to other residents. This lady is constantly looking for things she can do for others regardless of her medical issues and physical disabilities. Currently, she is crocheting a baby blanket for a pregnant staff member. Imagine the joy she will share with the parents when the baby is born.

If we have the concept and desire to do something good for others, we can always find the opportunities, no matter where we are, or what kind of condition we are in. Years ago we had a retired pastor and his wife at one facility. He served as a volunteer chaplain. She was a stroke survivor and could not speak. But wherever she went in her wheelchair, she had eye contact with people, holding their hands, listening to them, nodding her head. It was very moving to see how she continued to serve as a pastor's wife. She was not the only one who overcame the barrier for communication. One lady who cannot speak would just open her arms and give people hugs. It is inconvenient for most residents to physically go out to visit family and friends. But most people keep the communication going by phone calls or sending cards. One patient asked his wife to order flowers as gifts for people on special occasions.

Sometimes, opportunities come quickly and unexpectedly. You had better be ready any time. One patient resumed his Christian faith after praying with me. Two weeks later, he told a therapist how God had been helping him. At the end of the conversation he led his therapist to Christ. She actually said that simple prayer to invite Jesus as her Savior. That was so awesome! Not only that, about a month later he led an elderly resident to Christ. A young lady was born with HIV. The first time I visited with her, she told me she would like to be a motivational speaker down the road. A few weeks later the therapy department made arrangements for her to speak to children who were born with HIV at a children's hospital.

Sometimes, what you do may seem insignificant, but would mean a lot to the other person. One time while I was travelling I sat next to a lady on the airplane. The whole time she was reading a book about management. When I glanced over the book, it appeared to be for beginners. Finally the airplane was beginning to descend, preparing to arrive at our destination. She closed the book and started to chat with me. She said that she had worked in management position in the corporate world for many years. I said that I was surprised to hear that, because she looked young and the book seemed to be written for beginners. She appeared to be deeply touched. She told me that what I said meant a lot to her. Her birthday was coming up in just a few days and she had been feeling sad about it.

I hope you feel relieved that to fulfill this assignment is not hard and you are motivated to take actions to do good deeds whenever possible. I do need to caution you about one thing though. Avoid trying to benefit others by rendering constructive criticism. Let me tell you a very embarrassing thing I have done. When the weather is good I take a walk around our neighborhood just about every day. A few years ago, a house several blocks away had a sign up for sale. The house had beautiful rock siding and a reddish brown door and panels on both sides of each window to match

162

some of the rocks. To get it ready for sale the owners changed the color of the door and window panels to black. When I walked by it, I was thinking that they made a terrible mistake. A month went by and I started to think this color might make it harder for them to sell the house. Every time I walked by the house I had an urge to tell the owners about it. I did not know them. As time went on, I started to feel compelled by God to tell them. I was thinking what if they could not sell the house because I did not have the courage to give them such important feedback which their family and friends might be reluctant to give. Finally, one day I could not stand it anymore. I told myself that I had nothing to lose but it might be a

determining factor for their house sale. So, I
walked up to their door and rang the doorbell.
The lady of the house answered the door. I
explained to her what I thought about the color
of their door and window panels and why I
came up to tell her. Her simple response was,
"No, I don't think so." You are probably
laughing like crazy right now. Two weeks later,
the house was sold. I was wrong. I was so glad
when they actually moved away. Super
embarrassing!

Now, do you see what it means to be
human? A lot of things that we think we are
right and others are wrong are simply our own
opinions, not the absolute truth. In fact, there

is no absolute truth in a lot of things, only various opinions. I have had several patients whose children would not visit them nor talk to them. They had no clue why. I wondered if they had done something similar to what I did. Sometimes our good intentions do not exempt us from negative consequences.

But you do not have to get scared. If you just stick to the principle of being supportive and encouraging toward others, you will not mess things up. Show people appreciation and give them praise. Remember that God is love. (1 John 4:8) And love never fails. (1 Corinthians 13:8)

12.

GET MORE HELP AND KEEP LEARNING

I hope you have found the help you need from this book. If you have, encourage other people to read it too. Not only that, set it as a goal for you to encourage others by giving your testimony. Nothing is more powerful than the real experiences from real people. Nothing is wasted in life. Let your struggles strengthen you. Let your experiences enhance your life. You are a real winner.

Continue to learn in your daily living. We are surrounded by all kinds of people we can learn from. Practically everyone is our teacher. We learn what to do from positive

examples. We learn what not to do from

negative examples. People have more wisdom

than we give those credit. I asked my

hairdresser's son if longer hair would make

women look younger. He said that what made

a difference was the attitude, not the length of

hair. Sometimes people inspire us not by their

words, but by their presence. I am greatly

inspired by a young lady who works in the

kitchen at a nursing home. She is deaf. She is

not only hard-working but is also friendly and

pleasant all the time. I have a neighbor who

had a surgery to remove a brain tumor. After

the surgery he completely lost all his functions.

He had to learn everything all over like a baby.

A year later, he was mowing the lawn and doing

yard work again, although he was not

completely the same. I have told him he is my

hero. Every time when I see him pushing the

mower in their yard, I waive at him and give him

two thumbs up. That is a real winner on display.

Be alert and pay attention, so that you may not

miss out on learning opportunities.

Find other books to read. Watch

teachings on TV and online. There are many

wonderful teachers out there. We learn

different things from different people because

of the variety of expertise, knowledge, and

personalities. If possible, have fun with it. Have

discussions with your family and friends.

Mentor others when you get better at it. Form

a club or support group in your area with

people who are trying to overcome similar

problems. There are many, many things you

can do. Be creative. Help others be winners

too. This may be the last chapter of this book.

It should be a new chapter of your life. Enjoy

the journey.

But if you feel your problems are much

more complex and much greater than the scope

of this book don't be reluctant to seek

professional help. A self-help book is limited in

many ways. It may not be suitable for every

person and it cannot cover all ground. It has

been a great challenge for me to write it. A very

important lesson I have learned as a clinician is to truly embrace the attitude of not making assumptions about my patients. I constantly examine the patients case by case, always keeping an open mind that some new information may be revealed and the profile may change. Treatment plans are constantly revised according to the patient's changes and progress. A self-help book is taking a completely different approach, trying to make it relevant to people in all kinds of conditions and situations. I will not be surprised if I miss the mark for some readers.

First of all, if you have suicidal thoughts you definitely need professional help, even if the thoughts come and go. I would encourage you to make an appointment now. If this is not during the office hours and you feel really bad, please call the National Suicide Prevention Lifeline at 1-800-273-8255. They are available 24 hours a day, 7 days a week. But please do not substitute on-going therapy with occasional phone conversations with Lifeline's volunteers. You need to have face-to-face interaction with a professionally trained psychologist or counselor. In some cases, they may recommend that you see a psychiatrist also. Set aside your pride and apprehension. You will not be judged or put down. These people will help you with compassion. Give yourself a big pat on your back if you make the phone call to save your own life. I am proud of you.

Listen to your inner voice. If you have the same problem repeatedly and you cannot get rid of it, although you do not have suicidal thoughts, you may need professional help. You will get individualized treatment which may be more on target than just reading this book. I had a patient who repeatedly had extramarital affairs. Thankfully her husband had the wisdom that she needed professional help and was very supportive. She had been raped several times in her childhood and her youth. Therapy helped her heal her past traumas. She realized that her infidelity was her instinct to get even with men and to regain her sense of power and control.

Once she felt her inner healing had taken place

and she had obtained a sense of justice by

sharing her experiences with me, she felt she

was set free.

If you have one or more addictions,

most likely you need professional help.

Addictions may include alcohol, street drugs,

prescription drugs, cigarette smoking, food,

especially sugar, pornography, gambling,

workaholics, etc. Most people do not have

addictions simply because they failed to say no.

I have had a few patients who had good parents

and good families, no sexual, physical, or

emotional abuse experiences of any kind. They

got involved in drug abuse mainly because of peer influence in the neighborhood environments. Nevertheless, most people have much deeper and complicated issues underlying their addiction problems. Fighting addictions is a big battle. Even if you feel your addictions are pure and simple, you will benefit from specially trained professional help. Generally, I would refer my patients to receive addiction treatment if they come to the nursing homes only for short-term rehab due to medical issues. Be reassured that confidentiality is protected by law. The most important thing is that you need to be transparent in front of your therapist whether you have addiction or other issues.

They cannot be truly helpful to you if you don't allow them to truly know you.

If you have been sexually or physically abused, you also need to let your therapist know about that. I have come across quite a few patients who had long histories of psychiatric disorders and treatments but they never told any therapists about the abuse. Your therapist is supposed to ask you and invite you to talk about your history of being abused. If they don't ask you but you volunteer the information to make your therapy more on target and effective, you are a real winner. I know it takes a lot of courage to do so. By taking that step you are paving your way to

victory. You will not regret it.

Another thing you may need to take a

proactive approach is to help your therapist

understand your background, especially if you

are from a culture very different from your

therapist's. I am not telling you to give a

cultural introduction lecture. Just keep in mind

that you may need to explain certain things

from time to time. If you and your therapist

communicate with each other well, cross-

cultural counseling can be a rich and wonderful

experience. You will find that it is nice to

expand your horizon.

You may not be able to freely choose your therapist due to your insurance network or geographical distance. Make the best of what you can get. Keep in mind that making the best of what you get is also a very important life skill which may be exactly what you need to cultivate. The reality of life is that nothing is perfect in life. In fact, nothing is perfect in this world. People in management positions all know how important it is to use employees' strengths and to overlook some weaknesses when they don't matter. I used to work with a social worker whose office was always messy. But appearances can be deceiving. She was actually very organized. She was organized in her own way. She was one of the best social workers with whom I have worked.

It may take a while for you to get comfortable with your therapist. While you are trying to build a positive working relationship with your therapist, you are sharpening your social skills, communication skills, and skills for teamwork. These will all benefit you in your life. Keep in mind that effectiveness of therapy does not depend only on the therapist. It is teamwork.

On the other hand, if you have built a strong and positive working relationship with your therapist, remind yourself that it is a professional relationship, not a personal relationship. Do not anticipate people in your life to give you undivided attention like your therapist. It is not a fair comparison. Your therapist went to graduate school to learn and practice all the techniques to make you feel good during the sessions. In their personal lives, therapists are just regular people. I know because I am one of them.

If you really like your therapist, caution yourself not to let your therapy go on forever. Your goal is to get strong and independent to the point that you can stop visiting with your therapist. Just like the goal of parenting is to raise children to become functional, responsible, and independent adults, the goal of therapy is for the therapist to help people become functional, responsible, and independent. Talk to your therapist when you feel ready to stop your therapy. Do not simply drop out on your own. Premature termination of therapy may cause relapse.

Be careful not to cross the line and fall in love with your therapist. Counseling is a very unique setting where two people experience unusual intimacy. Sexual relationship with the patients is a big no-no for mental health professionals. This will cause your therapist to lose his/her license. In most cases, the patients are emotionally traumatized.

If you have chronic depression and/or anxiety, be sure to see a physician in addition to seeing a therapist. A lot of physical/medical issues may cause depression, anxiety, insomnia, and fatigue. You may be surprised to know what they find and can correct for you.

Ok, that is about all I can think of for now. Oh, yes, be sure that you tell your therapist that you have read this book. That way you can build upon some of the foundations that you have already established. Keep going. You will reach your goal.

It is my wish and prayer that everyone who reads this book is experiencing God's power and God's love. I pray that God heals you, mind, body, spirit, and soul. I pray that God gives you peace and restores your joy. I pray that God equips you and empowers you to be His instrument to bring His light and His love to people around you. Receive your healing and blessings now in Jesus' name. Amen.

Made in the USA
Columbia, SC
18 February 2019